JR-isms

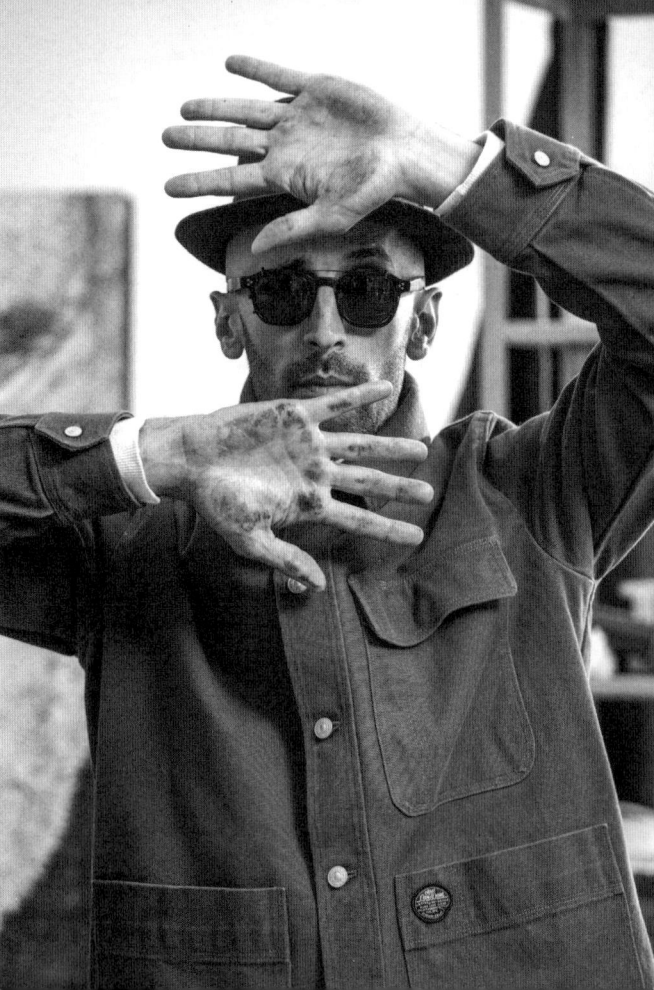

JR-isms

JR

Edited by Larry Warsh

PRINCETON UNIVERSITY PRESS
Princeton and Oxford

in association with
No More Rulers

Published by Princeton University Press,
41 William Street, Princeton, New Jersey 08540

In the United Kingdom: Princeton University Press,
99 Banbury Road, Oxford OX2 6JX
press.princeton.edu
in association with
No More Rulers
nomorerulers.com
ISMs is a trademark of No More Rulers, Inc.

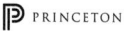 PRINCETON   NO MORE RULERS ®

All Rights Reserved
ISBN 9780691266299

Library of Congress Control Number: 2024936695
British Library Cataloging-in-Publication Data is available

This book has been composed in Johanna MT
Printed in China
1 3 5 7 9 10 8 6 4 2

CONTENTS

INTRODUCTION

Can art change the world? Many have asked this question, but few have pursued it as passionately as JR. Throughout his career, the French-born artist has understood that the creative response to that query is often a wholehearted "Yes." Using the urban environment as his canvas, JR's large-scale installations have redefined the role of public art and graffiti, not only in the art world but on the streets themselves. He invites whole communities into the creative reimagining of their neighborhoods, celebrating individual lives as well as collective accomplishments. He has an extraordinary ability to connect with the public, and that's essential to his success. His work is a poignant exploration of humanity, injustice, and the vibrant diversity of global communities.

From the suburbs of Paris to the slums of Brazil, from Liberia to Istanbul, from a maximum-security prison to the US–Mexico border, JR's artistic journey challenges societal norms and transforms public art into a powerful form of social dialogue. Born and raised on the outskirts of Paris, he began exploring the urban environment at a young age. Like many teenagers of his generation, JR saw graffiti as a way of making a personal mark on public space, and he enjoyed the adventure of tagging in risky settings. This early engagement with the streets of Paris and its many communities soon expanded to photography, and JR started his first major body of work—*Portrait of a Generation*—in 2004, when he was twenty-one. For this series, JR photographed teenagers and young adults from a housing project in the suburbs of Paris and pasted enlarged photocopies of their images on the sides of buildings and in the streets. He resumed the series two years later, after riots broke out over the deaths of two teenage boys from the neighborhood. Offering a different perspective from the media's portrayal of the youths, JR pasted the new images on the walls of the suburb and in wealthier parts of Paris.

The use of monumental scale has been a continuous thread throughout JR's career, reflected not only in the size of the works but the scope of the subjects. For *Women Are Heroes* (2008–14), he traveled to territories all over the globe, including Sierra Leone, Cambodia, India, and Brazil, to highlight the women who are often the primary victims of war and social unrest. Focusing on facial expression, especially the eyes, he captured an extraordinary range of complex emotions: strength, grief, dignity, anger, humor.

In 2011, JR took the entire world as his focus with Inside Out, an ambitious project launched after winning the TED Prize. In this ongoing series, creative control rests entirely with the participants, who submit their own stories, photograph themselves, and communicate their own experiences by pasting their portraits to create a work of public art. Since the launch of Inside Out, more than half a million participants from over 152 countries and territories have contributed, and others continue to add their voices to the project.

As an artist, JR has remained anonymous, downplaying his own identity to leave space for encounters between subjects and passersby. As with all books in the ISMs series, I hope to do the same here, to encourage a direct connection between reader and subject—in this case, JR as a thinker, creator, artist, and catalyst. In a world too often focused on the superficial trappings of success, JR has continued to reinvent the scope of artistic expression. He continually brings art to audiences well beyond the museum, turning public spaces into platforms for collective expression, dialogue, and social change.

In these pages, JR asks, "Can art change the world?" In one answer, he provocatively shifts the focus. "Maybe we should change the question," he suggests. "Can art change people's lives?" I believe wholeheartedly that it can—and perhaps JR's art most of all.

LARRY WARSH
NEW YORK CITY
JANUARY 2024

JR-isms

The Early Years

I came from an environment where there was no art at all. (3)

———

I didn't know Keith Haring or Basquiat or Cartier-Bresson. I didn't know there was a job of being an artist. (3)

———

I didn't know there was an art world. I didn't know that you could show in a gallery and that you could make movies. (5)

———

I didn't even know galleries existed. (11)

———

I think being naive is what has helped me the most. (3)

———

I may have more privilege now, but I didn't grow up privileged. (2)

———

I grew up in buildings where our neighbors were from all over the world. (11)

———

I've always been really close to old people. I grew up with old people—with my grandparents in the house and neighbors around. (22)

———

I wasn't the kind of kid who drew, and there wasn't any art on the walls at home, just a poster of Astérix and Obélix on a flying carpet, hanging in the living room. (7)

———

When I used to take the train, I was glued to the windows, watching the graffiti speeding by; no one else was looking. (7)

———

I was not the best student in my class, but I had great teachers. (44)

———

I was bored in class. I'd rather be engraving
my initials on desks. I didn't do it with
markers, but with a blade so that when the
desks were cleaned, my signature was
still there. (7)

I didn't spend enough time in school for
any of the teachers to remember me. The only
role models I had were the guys in the
neighborhood doing graffiti. (16)

I was hanging around outside by the age
of eleven. (7)

One of my neighbors was the leader of a very well-known graffiti gang called the ABCs. They remain an influence. This introduced me to graffiti. (1)

———

I wanted to follow those guys who were exploring the city, disregarding the law. (7)

———

I made tags, which doesn't require any incredible style, just a bit of attitude and the courage to climb out over rooftops and plunge into dark metro tunnels, and lots of time to spare. (7)

———

There's really no training for graffiti.
It's yourself. (39)

―――――

The calmer you are, the more guts you have,
the less you got in trouble. (11)

―――――

For a long time [graffiti] was called vandalism.
(4)

―――――

From the beginning, when I started carving
my name everywhere, it was a really simple
way to say, "I'm here, I exist." (7)

―――――

I had a lot of freedom in my family … they trusted me, I didn't have to sneak out. (7)

———

My parents slept in the living room, so it was like: "You can stay out as late as you want as long as you go to school and don't get in trouble." (11)

———

I found a camera in the subway in Paris. When I was a teenager, I followed graffiti artists who were older and more experienced than me. I was not as skilled, but with the camera, I could document their work. (1)

———

I never photographed the tags, but the guys who were doing them, in the heat of the action, on-site, in the metro tunnels, on rooftops. (7)

———

I wanted to capture the invisible atmosphere of the graffiti world: the electric ambiance of a dark tunnel, the speed of trains that pass just a few meters away as you're hiding. How to translate this atmosphere? (7)

———

I realized that graffiti was my passion and
that it allowed me to go anywhere, to Paris
or elsewhere. (7)

———

Growing up in the projects and living
through the riots that exploded at the time,
I saw the wall that was there. Even if it was
not physical, there was a wall between Paris
and the suburbs. That's what inspired me to
want to see what other kinds of physical or
virtual walls existed around the world and
how they shaped the perceptions that
we have of each other. (10)

———

Ever since the beginning, walls have been
my places of expression. (10)

———

Each time I've seen walls that have caught
my attention, they would stick in my mind.
I would even dream about them. (25)

———

I was respected in the world of graffiti,
but also had a foot in another world, that
of photography, of pasting. (7)

———

The only thing I knew about the art world was the photo gallery at the FNAC in Les Halles in Paris. I didn't know anything else. I had even submitted my work to exhibit there. It seemed to me that this gallery at the FNAC was the only option for a future in the arts. (7)

————

I pasted really early in the suburbs of Paris, and when the riots exploded [in 2005] I began to understand that a photo of my friend holding a video camera like a weapon can take on another meaning. (14)

————

In 2005, the guy from the [media] agency wanted to pay me to take photographs of the kids who were burning down the projects. [My friend] Ladj and I refused to work with him, instead suggesting that he print our first photos, the ones from before the riots; it was a provocation. And that's when I finally realized that I was an artist, not a photojournalist. I never looked back. (7)

———

JR stands for the fact that I'm still the same
kid who is trying to see the world from
different perspectives. I am the same now
as I was when I was 15 years old climbing
onto the rooftops of Paris and
the Paris suburbs. (13)

———

I didn't travel much when I was young, so
for me just going from the suburbs to Paris
was a journey. I feel like I'm still on that same
subway train that was taking me to Paris,
and I always want to go further. (12)

———

I'm still that same kid who was doing graffiti,
writing his name, and remaining anonymous.
(27)

―――――

People were calling us "vandals" and then
"street artists," and then "artists"—and I think
"artist" is what I've always been, in a way,
without knowing it. Now that I understand
the meaning of it, I feel proud to be able
to use that name. (12)

―――――

I was writing my names on walls to say
"I exist," then I started pasting pictures of
people with their names to say *they* exist. (3)

———

Now, as an adult, I can tell my mother
I am not a vandal but an artist. (16)

———

Artmaking, Anonymity,
and the Creative Process

I constantly push myself to go places where I don't know anything, into worlds that I've never heard about. (18)

———

If there's something I don't know, that's where I'll go. That's been my education, how I've learned new things. (7)

———

My lack of academic background has always prompted me to learn empirically. That is why I am interested in what people experience most of all. (41)

———

One thing that has fascinated me from
the very beginning is unpopulated places,
but within populated cities. (13)

———

I need to stay anonymous. I want the focus
to be on my work and on the people who
participate in the projects, not on myself.
I don't want the projects to be read
differently if my name is Muhammad,
Eli, or Peter. (38)

———

In my work, I've always used the fact that I would only get evicted or arrested, whereas someone from another country might go to jail for years for trying the exact same thing. I use that to go and work in different countries and install artworks in places where the local people can't. (12)

In some places, [my posters] are framed and hung on the wall of a living room; in others, they're torn up and trampled on the ground. (7)

I put my work in places where nobody knows me. Yes, it's giant, but there's nothing written on it. It's there for whoever wants to know. (3)

———

When we were in Cuba, we didn't see much graffiti, but thousands of little marks on walls with people's names. (4)

———

I am still fascinated by all the people who left a mark, even a small one on any wall or surface just to say they were there. (4)

———

My work is not about just one city, or a few cities where I'm actually welcome in galleries and museums—it's about creating work in different contexts, and unfortunately, this same work is seen as a crime in one place and as a piece of art in another. (12)

———

For years, I would be completely anonymous. But I realized that by not talking about the work, people would not understand the complexity of it, the layers. I wanted people to understand the subject's intention. (3)

———

When I take off my hat and my glasses, no one recognizes me; it's reverse anonymity. (1)

I don't sign my installations in the street. It's up to the spectators to question, to ask those around them if passersby know what the installation is. The exchange is part of the work. I seek to create as many interactions as possible. (1)

I like to say that my work is not illegal because even if I don't ask for authorization from the government, I ask the people. (15)

All I've been doing with my work is figuring out how to create more and more distance between myself and the projects so that it spurs conversations between people. (15)

———

I always make sure in my art that I even confront my own perspective. (18)

———

My aim was always to let the work speak for itself. (12)

———

What I try to capture in every installation
is a combination of pasting, photography,
getting people to physically move to see the
work, and encouraging people to share
it so it reaches others. (12)

———

A lot of my work is very visible—people can
go and see it, but it's ephemeral—I don't
write my name on it, there's no trace of
it at all after it's gone. (12)

———

For me, the pasting, the preparation, the
installation—all of this is the art. The photo
is the memory of it. I don't define myself
as a photographer. (1)

I'm always there for the pasting because that's my favorite part. (24)

———

I do huge posters because people shouldn't go to see the posters. The posters must be big enough so they can see it from afar. (38)

———

The eye has become my identity. (1)

———

The hand is also very important to me; it expresses what the eye can't say. (1)

———

I am part of the generation that has witnessed photography go from an expensive sport to being something that everyone can use. (14)

———

In this last decade, photography has become a daily practice that can be done by anybody, which is actually really interesting, and I am willing to use that in my work. (12)

———

Documentary films have always been a part of [my work], to capture people's reactions and record the impact of the projects. (7)

———

I've never had a sense of possession of my work; I've always been fine letting it disappear. (12)

The thing that keeps me going is creating with others. (41)

I'm independent, but I don't work alone. I need a team and to be involved in local communities because the projects are immense and one person is not always enough. (7)

When there is more chance of failure
than success in a project, something
amazing might happen. (1)

What worked for me was to be uninhibited
and to create as much as possible. (1)

As an artist, you have a responsibility,
right? (39)

Being an artist, you can't ever renounce the idea of believing in a better world. Agnès [Varda] certainly believed in that, and when I wake up in the morning, I don't give myself any other choice. (16)

———

If I put my art at the service of brands, what is the difference between art and advertising? (1)

———

I use black and white to differentiate from the color codes of advertising. (38)

———

Playing in the streets with giant images could look like advertising, except mine do not sell anything. They don't have any text on them, and I'm not even signing them. (21)

———

When people see my art, I want them to know it's not advertising. I'm not trying to sell you something through the story of this person. I want to keep these installations [as] a place where people can dream, where they can be inspired, where they can question. (32)

———

The only time I don't allow free copyright
is when brands use my work in their
own commercials. (15)

———

I don't want my projects to have a logo
on them. I've always wanted to keep that
freedom, which makes things much harder
because it's now one of the main funding
sources in the art world. (2)

———

Some people think the way the corporate
world does things is the only way, but there
are other ways. You just have to create them.
(15)

———

The way I finance my work is as important
as the message that we're carrying. (39)

———

The financing is a key part. You wouldn't
interpret my work in the same way if I did
it with a brand. (26)

———

Ninety-nine percent of my work is installed in
the streets around the world—it's free for the
people, they can take photographs and print
them at home if they want. Only 1% of what
I do finances that entire 99%. (12)

———

In galleries, I exhibit blueprints, plans, and preparatory sketches to show the process behind my projects. The final installation is shown through photographs and films. I've also designed mechanical artworks specifically for gallery spaces that recreate my installations on a smaller scale. (12)

———

I sell artworks based on each project, then this pays for the next one. (18)

———

In a way, the art market becomes a shadow philanthropist of my work without knowing it. ... I'm reinvesting the money I make with it to create more art, to actually install in the streets, to visit places where art has never happened, and to constantly spark conversations. (15)

———

Christo and Jeanne-Claude were the only artists I knew that really pushed self-financing to such a level. (39)

———

My work has always been about action. It's a
reality that we discuss as we watch it happen.
(14)

Once pasted, the art piece lives on its own.
The sun dries the glue and with every step,
people tear pieces of the fragile paper.
The process is all about participation of
volunteers, visitors, and souvenir seekers. (45)

When you think the artwork is finished, that's
actually when the journey is beginning. (40)

Sometimes I love when the process is a
bit longer, when the process is a bit more
complicated and involves more people.
It's more painful, but those become
the good stories after. (40)

———

I work with the individuals—they decide
how they want to be represented. (33)

———

Every person I have met and photographed,
or who has given me a photo of themselves,
has been part of my projects. (13)

———

I always work in a spirit of mutual trust,
especially because with my first lens, a 28mm,
I had to be really close to my subjects. (7)

———

I have no responsibility to anyone but
myself and the subject. (19)

———

Everything is about eye contact. (26)

———

I always come to a place naively, and I talk to
people so that I can understand the context.
I try to find a project that I can
create with them. (14)

———

We always make do with what is available,
that is the best method. (1)

———

I have few unrealized projects because I always
find a way to make them happen. (1)

———

At the end of the day, I wallpaper buildings.
That's what I do. So that's why I think the
title of "artist" is the most prestigious
title I'll ever get. (28)

———

As much as I'm a printer, I am a photographer,
I am a wallpaper man. (28)

———

In a way, I can never truly say that my work is done, because something out of my control can always happen, something that will give my work even greater meaning—or perhaps add nothing at all. I must always live with this doubt, with no absolute control over what might become of my work. (31)

———

I don't have a long-term project, but one project always leads to another one. (7)

———

The question people always ask me is,
"What's next?" It's really scary when you
work like that. There could be nothing next.
But I like being able to change direction
at any time. (17)

———

Ultimately, what drives me today is instinct.
(7)

———

Even now, I couldn't tell you what I'll do next
year. … I love not knowing. (17)

———

If you look at all of my projects from the beginning, they're all interconnected. They respond to each other. (12)

All my projects exist only because they mean something to the people involved. (41)

My main aim is to show the humanity in people. (16)

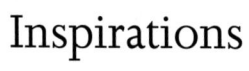

Inspirations

When I was a kid and all through adolescence,
I didn't have any artistic references or
knowledge. (7)

———

When I started seeing [walls] as a canvas,
my entire perception of the world
changed and suddenly every trip
was an exploration. (4)

———

Seeing anything from a different angle always
attracts me even if there is risk. (4)

———

Just to be able to change people's perception
of a place is a huge success for me. (12)

———

We expect artists to always be working in the
gray zone, always going where others don't.
(7)

———

I never tire of creating walls that ask passersby
questions. For example, what does this man
think of when he closes his eyes? What are the
first images that come to mind amongst the
millions that have marked his life? What will
my own wrinkles, which are in the process
of forming, say about my life? (34)

———

The street is the place where I have the
most interesting interactions. (4)

The streets have always been where an open,
constant discussion can take place that is
independent of any media and outside
of any political party. (15)

When I got into art, they would arrest me for
graffiti. ... I didn't see that as a crime. (6)

I have been to North Korea and could feel
that there was no democracy because the
walls were very clean—no graffiti,
no posters, nothing. (15)

———

In front of such a dreary place, a wall
separating peoples, life can be filled with joy,
hope, and light, if only for a moment—that's
something we need in order to live
and carry on. (31)

We need to remind people that the world is interesting because it's not just black and white. That's why I work in all those shades of gray. (18)

―――――

The image is the excuse for people to actually connect in the physical world. That's really important to me. (12)

―――――

The main catalyst in my work is to reconnect people. (5)

―――――

[There are] moments a little out of time, where reality meets the magic of an instant … and a picture suddenly takes on a whole new meaning. (31)

I know that walls are supposed to divide us, but I think I've found a way to use walls to bring us together. (37)

Photography may be the raw material in my artistic approach, but what I am most interested in is how it connects people, how it makes them interact and take part in the art. (41)

One of the first places I started working was in the tunnels of Paris; there is no one there, but there's the presence of people who have walked through, the energy of the people who built the tunnels. (13)

———

For me, the city is a playground—completely, fully, in every sense. (9)

———

I always let the architecture dictate the work. That's why [my pieces] fit in the environment like they belong there. (12)

———

I've always been curious to learn from older
people who are from different countries,
cultures, generations, and contexts, because
with a certain age comes a certain wisdom.
(22)

———

The narratives of other people have always
been more interesting to me than mine. (3)

———

I went from "I exist" to "they exist," then
I realized the power of that. (28)

———

[The 1995 film *La Haine*] was my first artistic
reference, my first inspiration. (1)

It's the strength of your message [that] makes
you as an artist successful. (39)

Each time I saw a film by Agnès [Varda] I felt
a sense of complete freedom in her way of
making them and in her way of living. When I
met her, I saw that it's not just how she makes
films, it's how she approaches life. (23)

Spending so much time with Agnès really taught me of the power of being inquisitive, no matter your age. (16)

———

[Agnès] was more curious than anyone I ever met, even at 90. Until her last day, right before she died, she was planning her next show. That is something people often misunderstand about our friendship; we considered ourselves the same age. (16)

———

It was really powerful for me to work
with dancers from the New York City Ballet,
because they're such professionals that if you
have an idea, they make it happen. If you have
no idea, they will make something happen.
(24)

———

Christo and Jeanne-Claude inspired me
the most. (1)

———

If a project seems too easy, it's not interesting.
(20)

I love when I start a day and I really don't know where it's going to take me. Waking up every day in a different country, creating projects, never really looking back, being in the action, maybe that's why I've always been documenting it, to keep a trace of it. It's not only about the art, it's about the people. (43)

———

I want to use art as a bridge to make people talk to each other. I'm not an activist, I'm just an artist. I don't try to tell people what to think. I just try to make them think. (37)

———

In my studio, I have a big sign that says
"It's going to be all right." So we have that in
front of us every day because most of the time
we're doing stuff that, on paper, isn't possible.
Sometimes it really isn't possible. But other
times you get surprised. (12)

———

Often, the limits are farther than we think. (1)

———

I love the surprises in life and in art. (21)

———

Community and Culture

I realized very early on that I was obsessed by the power of community. The process of making art together is actually far more interesting than the final piece. (16)

———

All of my work is centered on the involvement of the community, the people of all the social situations in all the cities. (29)

———

I've always grown up in a community setting. I've always shared everything. I've never had a sense of ownership. (7)

———

I'm just an enabler. It becomes [the people's] art project. (15)

———

By moving into the shadows of the media, the idea is to let the people who are participating in my projects, who make them possible, do the talking. (7)

———

Nothing could exist without collective mobilization. (41)

———

[The street is] the city's best gallery I could imagine [because] I never have to present my work to a gallery and let them decide if it is nice enough to show it to people. I control it directly with the people in the streets. (19)

———

I often work with no authorization and no sponsor. More important than the authorizations, I need the full support from the people who are on the posters. Often, I also get some kind of consensus from the people when they see the work-in-progress. (38)

———

I came from graffiti, so that's why I stayed semi-anonymous in the beginning, but I've never refused to speak about my work because I had to speak to the people in the street who were the actual curators, who decided if I could do my piece. (12)

———

I've often had to explain my work in very different contexts, and each time I have to justify myself for wanting to paste these black-and-white posters that don't always mean the same thing in different countries. (7)

The same black-and-white photo can
be a crime in one country and a piece
of art in another. (15)

———

The power of the image comes from the
location where it's pasted. (34)

———

Only in relation to others does identity
exist. (41)

———

I feel safe when I see graffiti because it shows there's life. When you go to countries and there's not one single tag on the wall, you should be stressed. (3)

———

To me personally, being born in France has helped me—it's allowed me to be on the Palestinian side and the Israeli side on the same day. For a lot of people that would be impossible. (12)

———

When it comes down to it, notions of borders and migration run right through my whole artistic corpus. (41)

———

I am always willing to participate in events that gather people physically together and where we can debate under the same roof. This is what we need in today's world where virtual and dematerialized technologies are taking up space over real and true relationships. (30)

———

You can very quickly get stuck in a bubble, especially now with social media, because everyone looks at the bubble that interests them, only follows the people they're interested in, and so only sees the part of the world that interests them. (7)

———

For me, art is about creating a bridge, one that connects with the community, and when that is in place, I pull myself out of the picture completely. (9)

———

I think it's people's curiosity that motivates them to participate in the projects. And then it becomes more. It becomes a desire, a need, an armor. (19)

———

The people in the street, they are the creators. (19)

———

The first thing I noticed was people's pride in seeing their pictures. They were grateful to be represented differently. (2)

———

These photographs, old or recent, cropped and enlarged, create a monumental artwork on the walls of the neighborhood and transform these personal memories into part of the collective history. (46)

———

It fascinates me to exhibit, as I did in Cuba, portraits of unknown people, in a country where the only portraits on the wall are those of leaders. (1)

———

I believe all people have amazing stories. (13)

———

Art lets us share something. When you're
a reporter, you go take a photo and never
come back. In our case, we go there and do
something with the people that we document.
It changes the whole dynamic because we all
shared something that we built together. (21)

———

I like to coordinate and connect actions that
symbolically link people from one continent
to another. I did that with *Women Are Heroes*
and *The Wrinkles of the City*. Each project
functions on its own, but it also connects
to a larger whole. (41)

———

It is important for me that the projects I create in one place live on elsewhere, fostering new encounters and resonances. (41)

That's the power of the project; [it's] not that the photos are beautiful, it's that it gathers community and it's those connections that actually create such an impact. (40)

Often, my illegal work is supported by the public and tolerated by the authorities. I have been told that the law of a country reflects the moral consensus of its citizens. So, when something illegal is tolerated, does it mean that this consensus is challenged? And that it can evolve? Or does it just mean that everybody knows that the wind will tear down the posters anyway? (38)

———

There have been moments where I have feared for my life. But I always believed in what I was doing because I did it in partnership with the community. (16)

———

Regardless of where the works are pasted, they have an impact. They are visible to all. (7)

———

Everyone's eye is unique, but we all find ourselves in the eyes of someone else. (1)

———

Dignity is connected to the way we're being seen by others, the way we portray ourselves. (28)

We all have something in common, we all want dignity, we all want respect. (13)

We all have that sense of, "I want to exist," of showing that we're here, that we're present. (28)

I've been to parts of the world where people's first priority was to put food on the table, yet, they would say to me, "We need art to restore our dignity; dignity is everything to us." (13)

———

Women are always the first ones targeted during conflict. (19)

———

What's interesting is if you talk to a woman in Brazil and a woman in Palestine, you realize that often they have the same point of view, they're being misportrayed, and they want to change that. (3)

———

Art is not supposed to change the world.
It can offer a new perspective, a new look,
break down the walls we build between us,
and humanize the "other." (1)

———

We forget that the "other" looks like us,
because every day, what we see in the media is
the terrorist or the soldier. It has a bigger
impact than I imagined. (1)

———

Showing another point of view, one that is not
negative as portrayed every day in the media,
changes public opinion and sows the seeds
of change in the community. (29)

———

What we see changes who we are. When
we act together, [it] is much more than the
sum of the parts. (19)

—

Are we living through a time of hatred?
No, I don't think so. I just think that hatred
is being amplified in a way that it
has never been before. (6)

—

Weirdly, when I go back to places where I pasted, even if the work is not there anymore, I talk to people and they talk about [the work], looking at the wall as if it's still there. … I think that's the power of the mind. We should not underestimate that power. (12)

———

As an artist, my role is not to manipulate numbers or deconstruct data; it is to highlight the human beings behind them. (41)

———

As an artist, I am not here to judge. Who am I to say we should change this or that? (16)

The power of an image, depending on the context, is such that the project can go on without me. It no longer belongs to me. (1)

———

I'm actually fine with [my work] being scratched, peed on, painted over, or whatever. It belongs to the people, and I have to let it go the minute I paste it. (15)

———

My work is really based on the power of community. I might be losing the final image, but I haven't lost the community. (6)

———

Life and Art

Art can go places, beyond roads, beyond rules, beyond borders, maybe because art is not part of any organization, it's not part of the state, it's something that we own, we the people own. And that's why it goes so far. (43)

———

Nowhere in the world has anyone told me there is no place for art. (41)

———

I've always felt like a citizen of the world. (11)

———

My artistic impulses are closely bound up with a desire to learn about the world around me, to understand it better. (41)

Surrounding yourself with people that come from different backgrounds, different stories, different paths, that's what nourishes us. (42)

Art can bring perceived opposites together. (47)

Art can change the perception we have of the world and perception is everything. There are people who don't like other people out of prejudice. It's only a perception. It's because they do not know each other well, they've never met. Art allows for a different vision of situations that we either don't understand or that we've seen only on television. (29)

We experience borders in completely different ways depending on where we were born. (12)

Sometimes art can have a great impact, and sometimes it does nothing. It's an experience where the artist searches for boundaries, where the artist tries to connect with people or make people think of something from a different angle. All those purposes of the artist are enough for me. (13)

———

If I ever have the potential to change the world, it would be in changing the perception we have of the world. (4)

We change the perception of the world by questioning it. By asking questions, we're able to push the boundaries. (14)

———

Can art change the world today? Absolutely, because it can change our perceptions of this world. (7)

———

[Art] helps change the way you see the world—and then, maybe, the actions you decide to take. (12)

———

I think my art is political just by the fact that it's in the street. (15)

———

My work has no borders. (24)

———

My art is about how we can break
down boundaries and reconnect with
each other. (8)

———

My work belongs to everyone as soon
as it exists. (31)

———

The biggest walls that we have are the
walls within us. (10)

———

It's a little weird for me to call it "street art" because we weren't calling it that when Basquiat and Haring were doing stuff in the streets. Now it's a popular name for it, but you don't call art in galleries "gallery art"—it's just art. (14)

———

For me, it's art whether it's inside or outside. Sometimes it doesn't work in a gallery. (3)

———

In the early years of my work, photography was at the beginning stages of being democratized by going digital. If I was born 15 years earlier, I might be doing something very different today. (13)

———

I never thought [my work] had to be illegal
to be good. If I could do everything
legally I would. (11)

———

I think art reflects things within us, within
one another. Some people decide to reflect
things that are more personal, while others
decide to express something more abstract,
which might reveal something in you,
but not in me. (14)

———

As an artist, you raise questions, but you
don't necessarily give answers. (10)

———

Art forces you to form your own opinion
about things. (7)

———

Behind each image is a story. (19)

———

To exist as an artist, there are a thousand paths.
Each person will find their own. (42)

———

You can fail as an artist, and I think that's
the strength. (20)

———

I like that as an artist you have this luxury to set your own codes; there are no rules and you have so much freedom. (9)

———

What I'm trying to do is really help artists figure out how to survive as an artist and make a living out of it, so they don't have to make the mistakes I have made. (10)

———

Those who gave me a studio in New York, they are my guardian angels, who do it for the impact of the art and not for any benefit they could receive in return. (7)

———

I think that one of the reasons why I live
[in New York] is because everyone is welcome
in a way here. It's a place where people ask
"Where are you from?" before "How
are you?" (20)

———

I don't let the heavy energy that can happen
around me impact my work. It's a mental
fight, but when you choose to be an artist,
you choose to fight all of your life. (16)

———

I am far more into practice than theory. (41)

———

I always recommend action, whatever the
cost and whatever the means. (1)

———

The only constraint I am under is urgency. (9)

———

I think as an artist you can easily fall into the
habit of doing the same thing over again.
I don't want to do that. (9)

———

I think there is no purpose of art aiming
for "success." It's a constant trial, and there
will always be artists pushing the limits,
and the limits will keep moving, and
we'll keep pushing them. (22)

———

My work might be famous, but I'm anonymous. (21)

———

I don't feel I've become well known. Most of the time I'm without my hat and glasses. It's a disguise, and if you take it off, then no one ever sees you. (5)

———

I never hide my eyes from people, only in front of a camera or in photographs. (12)

———

You know what they say, that the criminal always goes back to the crime scene? It works the same for the artist. When you do something in the street, you come back to see how people approach it. No one knows it's you, but you're right there. (27)

———

When social media appeared, I decided that I would publish everything directly, unfiltered. It's a way of sharing my thoughts live and to grant fewer interviews. (7)

———

Technology helps carry the stories; having them go to [new] places is the next step of the artwork. (41)

———

While working on all these projects, it struck me that sometimes, even in extreme situations, people rely on humor, because that's what makes them feel human and alive. (7)

———

With humor, there is life. (26)

———

If I go to a country and the streets are clean with zero graffiti, then that tells me the people are unable to express themselves. (16)

———

In moments like now, where everything has to be a fact, we leave less space for wonders. (6)

———

Before changing the world, change the world around yourself. (18)

———

Can art change the world? Maybe we should change the question. Can art change people's lives? (36)

———

The fact that art cannot change things makes it a neutral place for exchanges and discussions. This enables it to change the world. (19)

———

For me, changing the perception of a place, or people, or things is already a way of changing the world. And I think that art does that brilliantly. (15)

———

When I travel for my different projects, and I visit the local museums, I encounter beautiful murals that represent times that I haven't known, realities from another era. (33)

———

Now, more than ever, we have to open up the museums. This is supposedly a closed and elitist world. But if we open this world, we can change the rules. (7)

———

Sometimes I wonder, as an artist, why am I involved? I don't have a final answer but maybe the role of an artist is to make art, beauty, taste, emotions available to everyone. (48)

———

I have a duty to stay not only optimist[ic]
but almost utopist[ic], because as an artist, we
have to dream of something that is even non-
conceivable. And sometimes it actually
works and that's the beauty of it. (40)

———

Perhaps I am naively invested in the idea
of utopianism, but if, as artists, we lose that
utopianism, then I think the world
becomes lost. (16)

———

I would say the question is, how did I
even end up in the contemporary art world?
Chance is the only answer I can come up with.

(41)

———

Sometimes we underestimate the power of art.

(15)

———

Yesterday is yesterday, today is today, and
that's what we'll work with. (7)

———

I'm an artist until I find a real job. (18)

———

SOURCES

1. Obrist, Hans Ulrich, and JR. "JR & Hans Ulrich Obrist
    Interview." In *Artist Until I Find a Real Job*, edited by JR,
    23–40. Paris: Atelier JR, 2023.

2. Capelle, Laura. "All the World's a Canvas." FT *Weekend*,
    November 8, 2020.

3. Lakin, Max. "JR's Street Gallery Comes Indoors." *New York
    Times*, December 13, 2019.

4. Parlá, José. "Rebel, Rebel." *Cultured Magazine*, July 25, 2016.

5. Pener, Degen. "Artist JR on His New Documentary *Paper
    & Glue* and the Transformative Power of Art." *Hollywood
    Reporter*, November 20, 2021.

6. Harvey, Chris. "'At first, they used to arrest me …'" *Daily
    Telegraph*, October 31, 2020.

7. Bousteau, Fabrice, Hugo Vitrani, and JR. "The Retrospec-
    tive Interview." In *Retrospective JR: Chronicles*. Paris: Beaux
    Arts Editions, 2020. Published following the exhibition
    JR: Chronicles at Saatchi Gallery, London, June 4–October 3,
    2021.

8. Zack, Jessica. "Artist of the People." *San Francisco Magazine*,
    May 2019.

9. Coop, Elizabeth. "The Elusive Artist Using the Streets as an
    Art Gallery." *Dazed*, January 15, 2018.

10. Da Silva, Chantal. "'Walls Were My Places of Expression':

Street Artist JR on Turning Border Walls into Canvases."
The Independent, November 4, 2020.

11. Harvey, Chris. "The Rise of JR: How a French Graffiti Artist with a Xerox Conquered the Art World." *The Telegraph*, January 6, 2018.

12. Graham, Annabel. "JR: The Renowned French Artist Speaks." *Juxtapoz Magazine*, 2018.

13. Shoan, Tatijana. "Why Anonymous Street Artist JR Is the Next Banksy." *As If Magazine*. https://www.asifmag.com/story/jr-street-artist-artwork-interview.

14. Laster, Paul. "JR Tests the Ethical Side of the Art System." *Conceptual Fine Arts*, November 19, 2018.

15. Schumann, Sven. "JR: Power to the People." *Purple Magazine*, Issue 25, Spring/Summer 2016.

16. Hobbs, Thomas. "Backdrops to a Riot: JR on How His Confrontational Street Art Went Global." *The Guardian*, June 7, 2021.

17. Cadwalladr, Carole. "JR: 'I realized I was giving people a voice.'" *The Guardian*, October 11, 2015.

18. Duffy, C. "How to Unite People through Art (with JR)." In *How to Be a Better Human*. TED Audio Collective Transcript, June 27, 2022. https://www.ted.com/podcasts/better-human-how-to-unite-people-through-art-with-jr-transcript.

19. JR. "My Wish: Use Art to Turn the World Inside Out." *TED Talks*, March 2011.https://www.ted.com/talks

/jr_my_wish_use_art_to_turn_the_world_inside
_out?language=en.

20. Ang, Raymond. "French Guerilla Artist JR on Why Failure Yields Great Work." *Wall Street Journal*, October 4, 2019.

21. Goldberg, Peter. "Interview: Agnès Varda and JR on Finding the Art in Life with *Faces Places*." *Slant Magazine*, October 11, 2017.

22. Kim, Eugene. "Interview: Street Artist and TED Prize Winner JR." *My Modern Met*, August 4, 2015.

23. Kramer, Gary M. "Collective Enthusiasm: An Interview with Agnès Varda & JR." *Bomb Magazine*, October 6, 2017.

24. Pasori, Cedar. "Interview: JR Discusses His Art Series Collaboration with the Dancers of the New York City Ballet." *Complex*, January 23, 2014.

25. Schwartz, Alexandra. "The Artist JR Lifts a Mexican Child Over the Border Wall." *New Yorker*, September 11, 2017.

26. Day, Elizabeth. "The Street Art of JR." *The Guardian*, March 7, 2010.

27. Harris, Tony. "Guerilla Artist JR." *Al Jazeera America*, May 13, 2015.

28. Cooper, Anderson. "Art on 60 Minutes: JR." *CBS News*, 2018. https://www.cbsnews.com/video/art-on-60 -minutes-jr/.

29. JR. "JR in Conversation with Monica Bartocci." By Monica Bartocci. *RAI Radio Live*, October 12, 2020.

30. McMurtrie, John. "French Idea Translated: A Long Night of

Thinking." *San Francisco Chronicle*, January 30, 2019.

31. Cadiou-Diehl, Victoria. "Memories: JR's Souvenirs." City *Magazine*, May 2019.

32. Anders, Michael. "ICONIQ Ideas: Artist JR on How Creativity and Art Can Inspire Action." *ICONIQ Capital*, February 15, 2023.

33. JR, and Neal Benezra. *JR: The Chronicles of San Francisco.* San Francisco: Chronicle Books, 2019.

34. JR, Nato Thompson, and Joseph Remnant. *JR: Can Art Change the World?* London: Phaidon Press, 2019.

35. JR (@jr). Instagram, November 17, 2019.

36. JR. "One Year of Turning the World Inside Out." *TED Talks*, March 2012.

37. JR. "Why Art Is a Tool for Hope." *TED Talks*, April 2022.

38. JR / 28 *Millimètres*. Lazarides Gallery, January 1, 2008.

39. JR and Larry Warsh in conversation. New York City, May 12, 2023.

40. JR and Charles Melcher. "JR Reality and the Power of Portraits." *Future of StoryTelling*. June 1, 2023. Podcast, MP3 Audio, 31:36.

41. Galansino, Arturo. "Interview with JR." In JR: *Déplacé·e·s*, edited by Arturo Galansino, 9–19. Milan: Skira, 2023.

42. JR, dir. *Paper & Glue*. 2021. New York: MSNBC.

43. JR, dir. *Paper & Glue* (official trailer). 2021. New York: MSNBC. https://www.youtube.com/watch?v=14HEbf1p0Z8.

44. JR (@jr). Instagram, October 19, 2020.
45. JR (@JRart). Twitter, March 31, 2019.
46. JR (@jr). Instagram, March 8, 2019.
47. JR (@jr). Instagram, October 21, 2019.
48. JR (@jr). Instagram, March 16, 2021.

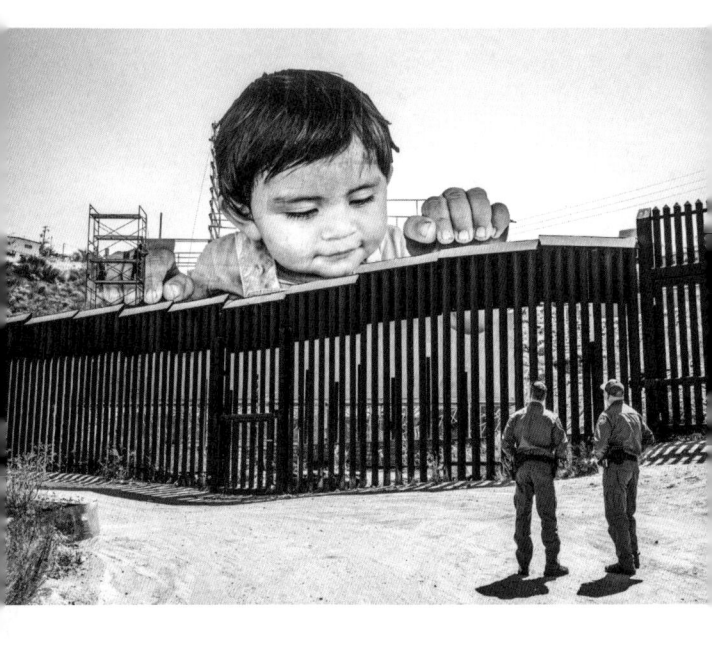

CHRONOLOGY

1983–2004

1983: JR is born in 1983 in the outskirts of Paris.

1996: He starts out as a graffiti tagger using the moniker Face 3.

2000: He transitions into photography after finding an old film camera in the Charles de Gaulle–Étoile station of the Réseau Express Régional (RER; the Paris Métro suburban railway system) and starts taking black-and-white photos of his friends while they are tagging.

2001: He begins exhibiting his photographs by pasting them on the walls of Paris and in the RER in an ongoing outdoor exhibition, Expo 2 Rue, from 2001–4.

2004: He begins Portrait of a Generation, his first large-scale street-pasting project, and he makes a short video called Clichés du Ghetto with his friend Ladj Ly.

2005

JR self-publishes his first publication, Carnet de Rue (My Street Diary), begun in 2004, which charts his practice and projects to date. It is a photographic narrative of the movement exploring the work of many artists, including Blu, Zevs, Banksy, Shepard Fairey, Bast, and Faile.

Riots break out in the outskirts of Paris in November, and JR's pastings in Les Bosquets are in the backdrop of news reports on the riots in the Montfermeil commune.

JR returns to the *Portrait of a Generation* project, transporting the images of young people out of the banlieues of Clichy-sous-Bois and Montfermeil by pasting them in bourgeois areas of Paris.

2006

JR covers the walls of the Maison Européenne de la Photographie in Paris with posters from *Portrait of a Generation*. He also pastes *Portrait of a Generation* photos on the outer walls of the Espace des Blancs Manteaux and on billboards around the Hôtel de Ville.

JR is part of a group exhibition at the Milk Gallery.

JR travels with his friend Marco Berrebi to Israel and the Palestinian territories to start the project *Face 2 Face*.

JR creates a sidewalk gallery with images from *Portrait of a Generation* at 11 Spring Street in New York City.

2007

Hoping to show the fundamental similarities and shared humanity among Israelis and Palestinians, JR and fellow artist Marco embark on the *Face 2 Face* project. They photograph Israelis and Palestinians from similar professions making funny faces and then enlarge and paste the juxtaposed black-and-white portraits in prominent places on both sides of the security barrier.

At the 52nd Venice Biennale, JR pastes *Face 2 Face* images on the front of the Arsenale building.

JR pastes images on the facade of the Foam Museum of Photography in Amsterdam and on two other sites in the city, along with a video installation.

JR participates in an outdoor exhibition at the Atelier des Forges during the Rencontres d'Arles in France.

JR has an exhibition on four building fronts and a video installation at Artitud in Berlin.

JR and Italian artist Blu collaborate on a mural for Planet Prozess 2007 in Berlin.

In an outdoor exhibition, JR pastes images on the facade of the Caserne Napoléon in Stravinsky Square and at the Saint-Merri school in Paris.

A special issue of the French daily newspaper *Libération* is devoted to JR.

The award-winning documentary film *Faces*, directed by Gérard Maximin, is released. It is about JR and Marco's collaboration in the Middle East in the *Face 2 Face* project.

2008

JR embarks on the *Women Are Heroes* project with the first action being exhibited in the Morro da Providência favela in Rio de Janeiro, Brazil.

Women Are Heroes actions take place in Freetown and Bo City, Sierra Leone; Monrovia, Liberia; and in the Sudan.

JR participates in the group exhibition *Street Art* at Tate Modern in London with an enormous pasting on the facade of the museum and additional images exhibited around the city.

JR's 28 Millimètres, *Women Are Heroes*, Rispah Atemba, Sierra

Leone, appears in the *Outsiders* exhibition in the Outsiders Gallery in London.

He begins *The Wrinkles of the City* project in Cartagena, Spain.

In an outdoor exhibition, JR displays images on two building fronts in Geneva during the International Film Festival and Forum on Human Rights, along with a video installation at the Musée Rath in Geneva.

JR's *Women Are Heroes* photographs are exhibited outdoors around the city of Brussels, Belgium.

2009

Women Are Heroes actions take place in Kenya, where two thousand square meters of rooftops are covered with photos of the eyes and faces of the women from the Kibera slum; in Jaipur, India, during the Holi Festival of Colors; and in Phnom Penh, Cambodia, for women fighting against the expropriation of their land.

JR returns to Brazil to paste images from *Women Are Heroes, Brazil* on the Arcos da Lapa monument. The Casa França-Brasil hosts video installations of the project and an opening with the participants from the favela.

The Casa Amarela opens, a cultural center offering art
classes for children and legal counseling for adults in
the Morro da Providência favela, where the *Women Are
Heroes* action took place.

JR participates in the Rencontres d'Arles photo festival in
France, exhibiting at the Ateliers SNCF.

After being invited by the Pavillon de l'Arsenal in Paris,
JR completes a large-scale exhibition of *Women Are
Heroes* on the banks of the Île Saint-Louis and the
Louis-Philippe bridge.

2010

The *Women Are Heroes* film premieres at the Cannes Film
Festival during Critics' Week.

JR participates in the Images Festival in Toronto, Ontario,
and in the Musée de l'Elysée de Lausanne in Vevey,
Switzerland, and begins the *Unframed* project.

JR participates in the Shanghai Biennale with *Wrinkles
of the City* actions in Shanghai, in collaboration with
Magda Danysz Gallery, and simultaneously puts up
photos illegally across China.

JR is included in a group exhibition at Galerie Springmann in Düsseldorf, Germany.

JR pastes images on the facade of the Museum of Contemporary Art, San Diego, and on other buildings
in San Diego for the exhibition *Viva la Revolución: A
Dialogue with the Urban Landscape*.

2011

JR receives the TED Prize, which offers him the opportu-
nity to make "a wish to change the world." He is the
first French person, the first artist, and the youngest
ever to receive the award.

JR initiates the Inside Out project, an international
participatory art project that allows people world-
wide to have their picture taken and paste it to
amplify a message.

The first Inside Out group action happens in Tunisia,
right after the revolution.

The documentary film *Women Are Heroes* is released in
cinemas.

JR's solo exhibition *Encrages* is displayed at Galerie

Perrotin in Paris. Massive Attack opens the exhibition with a concert.

The Inside Out Photobooth installation is in the *Paris-Delhi-Bombay* exhibition in the Centre Pompidou in Paris.

A *Wrinkles of the City* action takes place in Los Angeles.

JR participates in the *Art in the Streets* exhibition at the Museum of Contemporary Art in Los Angeles.

JR builds an Inside Out Photobooth in the foyer of Manarat Al Saadiyat for the opening of the *Emirati Expressions* exhibition in Abu Dhabi.

Three Inside Out Photobooths are installed in Bethlehem, Ramallah, and Israel.

2012

A *Wrinkles of the City* action takes place in Havana in collaboration with Cuban American artist José Parlá for the 11th Havana Biennial.

A year after winning the TED Prize, JR gives a TED talk on what has happened within a year in the Inside Out project.

An Inside Out action is installed on the High Line in New York.

JR travels to North Korea and captures images of Kim Il Sung's 100th birthday celebrations.

An Inside Out Photobooth is installed in Vevey, Switzerland, as part of the Images Festival.

An Inside Out action begins in Hong Kong on the Connaught Road footbridge in the city center.

JR's solo exhibition *Pattern* is displayed at Galerie Perrotin in Hong Kong.

An *Unframed* action begins in Washington, DC, using civil rights–era photographs.

A global Inside Out group action, called *Be the Change*, is about issues linked to climate change. More than four thousand posters are sent to seventeen cities across the world.

JR initiates a project in the areas of northeast Japan that are afflicted by the earthquake, the tsunami, and the nuclear disaster of Fukushima, and leaves an Inside Out Photobooth truck in the care of a group of Japanese artists, including Takao Shiraishi.

2013

JR's first museum retrospective, entitled *JR*, opens in Tokyo at the Watari Museum of Contemporary Art with a pasting on the facade representing inhabitants from northeast Japan, where the tsunami hit in March 2011.

JR and José Parlá return to Havana, Cuba, to give books to the participants of *Wrinkles of the City, La Habana*. The film *Wrinkles of the City: Havana, Cuba* is screened at Centro Cultural Fresa y Chocolate.

A JR app for the iPad is released, as well as a *Wrinkles of the City, Los Angeles* iBook for the iPad in English, Spanish, and French.

A *Wrinkles of the City* action begins in Berlin, along with a simultaneous exhibition at Galerie Springmann.

The documentary film *Inside Out: The People's Art Project*, directed by Alastair Siddons, premieres at the Tribeca Film Festival in New York City.

The exhibition *Wrinkles of the City, Havana* opens at Bryce Wolkowitz Gallery in New York City.

An *Unframed* action begins at Belle de Mai in Marseilles, France, in which JR asks residents to dig into their

personal photo albums and create a monumental
artwork on the walls of the neighborhood.

To commemorate the fiftieth anniversary of the March
on Washington, an *Unframed* action begins in Atlanta,
Georgia, where civil rights–era photographs are
pasted in the neighborhood where Martin Luther
King Jr. grew up.

JR returns to Kibera, Kenya, for another *Women Are Heroes*
action. Four thousand square meters of images representing the faces of women from Kibera are printed
on vinyl and installed on roofs to help protect communities from the rain. Since the initial pasting, a
team has returned three times to cover more rooftops
in Kibera.

JR, the first solo museum exhibition in the United States,
opens at the Contemporary Arts Center in Cincinnati,
Ohio.

An Inside Out Photobooth truck is installed in Times
Square. Six thousand people participate, and a three-
minute film is shown every night on Times Square
screens for Midnight Moment, the world's largest
and longest-running digital public art program.

Two Inside Out Photobooth trucks roam the United States during the summer to show the faces of eleven million undocumented immigrants and people pushing for immigration reform.

The first European Inside Out Photobooth truck travels to Amsterdam for the Unseen Photo Fair. Almost 1,800 posters are printed and pasted throughout the city.

JR's solo exhibition *Actions* opens at Lazarides Gallery in London, featuring work from *Wrinkles of the City, Berlin*; and a *Portrait of a Generation* action takes place at the site of the original project prior to the demolition of the buildings.

Inside Out Photobooth trucks are installed at Somerset House in London and at the Palais de Tokyo and the Bibliothèque Nationale de France in Paris.

2014

The *Inside Out* exhibition and an Inside Out Photobooth truck installation takes place at Dallas Contemporary in Dallas, Texas.

JR, a major retrospective exhibition at Museum Frieder

Burda in Baden-Baden, Germany, is accompanied
with a special Inside Out Photobooth installation.

An *Unframed* action in Baden-Baden, Germany, addresses
German-French history using archival photographs
from residents' private photo albums.

A massive installation by JR opens at Lincoln Center
for the 2014 New York City Ballet Art Series: an
eye, made with the dancers from the company, is
pasted onto the floor; a large pasting is also done on
the front windows of the David H. Koch Theater at
Lincoln Center.

JR creates the ballet *Les Bosquets* in collaboration with the
New York City Ballet, with music by Woodkid, and
is presented at Lincoln Center during XXIst Century
Week.

The major retrospective *Close Up* by JR is exhibited at the
Power Station of Art in Shanghai.

A solo exhibition showing new photos, wood, and
paper works by JR opens at Magda Danysz Gallery in
Shanghai.

An Inside Out Photobooth truck travels around Shanghai
for two months, resulting in pastings across the city.

The Inside Out installation *Au Panthéon!* opens to the public at the Panthéon in Paris.

The film *Wrinkles of the City: Havana, Cuba*, directed by JR and José Parlá, is released.

A *Women Are Heroes* action begins in Le Havre port outside Paris: 2,600 strips of paper are pasted onto shipping containers in Le Havre with the help of dockers from the port. The containers form a pair of eyes on a 363-meter-long ship leaving Le Havre for Malaysia.

An *Unframed* action begins in the derelict hospital on the south side of Ellis Island in New York, where millions of immigrants to the United States passed through from 1892 to 1954.

A photograph of JR's eye-strip posters depicting Eric Garner at a march against police brutality appears in the *New York Times*.

Rivages, a film by Guillaume Cagniard, about JR's pasting on a container ship in Le Havre, France, is released.

2015

JR's eye-strip posters of a *Charlie Hebdo* contributor who was killed during the attacks of January 11 appear at the front of the "Je Suis Charlie" march in Paris.

Coinciding with Art Basel, JR exhibits *JR: A Survey Exhibition* at the Hong Kong Contemporary Art Foundation and *Ghosts of Ellis Island* at Galerie Perrotin in Hong Kong.

The short film *Les Bosquets*, featuring ballet dancers from the Paris Opera Ballet in Paris, premieres at the Tribeca Film Festival in New York City.

Walking New York, a special issue of the *New York Times Magazine*, is published in collaboration with JR, and JR releases his first virtual reality short film about the project.

A *Wrinkles of the City* action begins in Istanbul.

JR's giant mural installation *Migrants, Ibrahim, Mingora-Philadelphia* begins in Philadelphia.

The film *Ellis*, directed by JR and starring Robert De Niro, premieres at the New Yorker Festival. Shooting is done in the abandoned Ellis Island Hospital complex.

During this year, JR has solo shows, including *Ellis* at Galerie Perrotin, Art Basel Miami and at Galerie Perrotin on the Lower East Side in New York City;

Decades at Galerie Perrotin in Paris; *Crossing* at Lazarides Gallery in London; and *Uprising* at CAC Málaga in Spain.

JR is the main guest artist of the 2015 Toronto Nuit Blanche.

JR collaborates with Darren Aronofsky on the major public artwork *Standing March* in Paris during COP 21 (United Nations Climate Change Conference).

2016

JR is artist in residence of the 2016 Rio Olympics and creates the installations *Giants* and *Inside Out Rio 2016*.

JR au Louvre, an installation on the pyramid of the Louvre Museum, is displayed in Paris.

JR's solo exhibition *You Are Here* begins at Centre Pompidou in Paris.

2017

JR's solo exhibition *Chroniques de Clichy-Montfermeil* opens in Palais de Tokyo in Paris; he also exhibits *Répertoire*, a solo museum retrospective in Qatar Museums Gallery in Katara.

The French documentary *Faces Places*, codirected by JR with Agnès Varda, wins the L'Œil d'or award at the Cannes Film Festival and is nominated for Best Documentary Feature at the 2018 Academy Awards.

JR and his team create the *Kikito, Giant* installation in Tecate, Mexico, at the US–Mexico border fence, followed by a picnic at the border.

The feature film *Chroniques de Clichy-Montfermeil*, directed by JR and Ladj Ly, is produced.

JR collaborates with Arcade Fire, U2, M, and Ibeyi.

JR's solo show *The Wrinkles of the City, Istanbul—Body of Work* is exhibited at Springmann Gallery in Berlin.

Mind the Gap becomes a permanent installation at Château La Coste.

JR creates Inside Out/Education and Inside Out/Dreamers, nationwide initiatives that seek to build a portrait of America that reflects its true diversity. During this time, Inside Out Photobooth trucks tour throughout the United States, emphasizing issues surrounding education and immigration.

2018

During this time, JR's solo shows include *Giants—Body of Work* at Lazinc in London; *So Close* at the Armory Show in New York City; *Amor Fati*, an installation at J1 in Marseilles; *Horizontal* at Perrotin in New York City; and *Momentum*, a major solo museum show at Maison Européenne de la Photographie in Paris.

JR creates installations for Refettorio Paris, a community kitchen located in the crypt of the church of la Madeleine, involving artists, designers, and chefs.

JR, working with *Time* magazine, creates the video mural *The Gun Chronicles: A Story of America*, which is presented in twelve museums around the United States and at Pace Gallery in New York City. It is also the cover image for *Time* magazine's special issue *Guns in America*.

Inside Out/Vote is created with the goal of reimagining civic engagement and mobilizing youth to vote. Inside Out Photobooth trucks tour throughout the United States to encourage people to register to vote before the midterm elections.

JR's *Giant* is installed on the Brandenburg Gate in Berlin
    for the German Unity Day, which celebrates the
    reunification of the country on October 3, 1990.

2019
During this year, JR's solo shows include *Unveiling* at
    Perrotin in Seoul, South Korea; *The Chronicles of San
    Francisco—Sketches* at Pace in Palo Alto, California;
    The Chronicles of New York City—Sketches at Perrotin
    in New York City; *The Chronicles of San Francisco* at
    SFMOMA; *JR: Chronicles* at the Brooklyn Museum;
    and *Patamar* at Galeria Nara Roesler in Rio de Janeiro,
    Brazil.
JR creates *Tehachapi, The Yard* mural at the California Cor-
    rectional Institution. The mural is included on the
    "JR:murals" app.
For the thirtieth anniversary of the Louvre Pyramid, JR
    creates *JR au Louvre & le secret de la grande pyramide*. More
    than four hundred volunteers collaborate with JR in
    pasting two thousand strips of paper, resulting in the
    largest pasting to date.

2020

JR creates *Tehachapi, Mountain*, his second installation at the California Correctional Institution.

Tehachapi, a solo exhibition, opens at Perrotin in Paris.

JR's artwork is featured on the covers of *Time* magazine's special issue *Finding Hope* and the *Così Sara* issue of *Vanity Fair Italia*.

JR's solo exhibition *Omelia Contadina* opens at Galleria Continua in San Gimignano, Italy.

Omelia Contadina, a short film by JR and Alice Rohrwacher, is presented at the Venice Film Biennale (Mostra).

JR installs *Arte em Campo* at Pacaembú Sports Complex in São Paulo, Brazil; the group show is a collaboration with Galleria Continua and Galeria Nara Roesler.

JR creates the set design and costumes for the ballet *Brise-Lames* at the request of choreographer Damien Jalet at the Paris Opera.

The *Homily to Country* is installed at the National Gallery of Victoria Art Triennial in Melbourne, Australia.

2021

Throughout the year, JR creates the following installations: *La Ferita* on the facade of the Palazzo Strozzi in
Florence; *Punto di Fuga* on the facade of the Palazzo
Farnese in Rome; *Les Falaises du Trocadéro* in front
of the Eiffel Tower in Paris; *No Trespassing*, for the
twentieth anniversary of the Parcours Saint-Germain;
Greetings from Giza, at the pyramids in Egypt and the
first NFT project; and an installation with Timothée
Chalamet at the Frick Collection in the Breuer building during the Met Gala.

JR's solo exhibitions during this year include *JR: Eye to the
World* at Pace Gallery in London; *Tehachapi* at Pace Gal-
lery in New York City; *Black and White* at Simon Studer
Art in Geneva; and *Contretemps* at Perrotin in Tokyo.
He also curates the exhibition *Truc à faire* at Galleria
Continua in Paris.

The award-winning film *Paper & Glue*, directed by and
starring JR, premieres at the Tribeca Film Festival in
New York City.

JR: Chronicles travels to Saatchi Gallery in London and to
the Groninger Museum in Groningen.

2022

JR and his team create *Déplacé·e·s, Valeriia*, a 45-meter-long tarp covered with the image of five-year-old Ukrainian Valeriia. Volunteers march through Lviv, Ukraine, while carrying the tarp overhead. A drone photograph from above is the cover of *Time* magazine (March-April issue). Images of Valeriia become two NFTs that raise funds for Ukraine.

Déplacé·e·s, Valeriia is an installation in the exhibition *This Is Ukraine: Defending Freedom* at the Venice Biennale.

JR creates *Tehachapi, The Road*, his third installation at the California Correctional Institution. The installation is accompanied by a picnic and the first-ever Inside Out Photobooth action in a prison.

JR gives his third TED talk, "Why Art Is a Tool for Hope."

JR: Chronicles travels to Kunsthalle München in Munich.

A two-week Inside Out Photobooth action takes place in Kobe, Japan.

JR and his team create *Déplacé·e·s, Rwanda*, a 45-meter-long tarp covered with the image of eight-year-old Thierry, who lives in the Mugombwa refugee camp. Children and adults carry the tarp through the area, and the procession culminates in a picnic and an Inside Out action at Mugombwa refugee camp.

As in Ukraine and Rwanda, JR and his team create Déplacé·e·s, Mauritania, a 45-meter-long tarp covered with the image of child refugee Jamal. Children and adults carry the tarp into the open desert and place it on the sand, where the children play together on top of it. The procession culminates in a picnic and an Inside Out action at Mbera refugee camp.

A pyramid-shaped Inside Out Photobooth is part of Art D'Égypte's installation exhibition Forever Is Now II by the Giza pyramid complex.

Participatory installations of Women, Life, Freedom begin in Rio de Janeiro, Brazil, and on Roosevelt Island, New York.

JR and his team create Déplacé·e·s, Colombia, a 45-meter-long tarp covered with the image of six-year-old Venezuelan refugee Andiara. More than two hundred children and adults carry the tarp from the basketball court to the soccer field in their neighborhood. The procession culminates in a picnic and an Inside Out action in Las Delicias by the Colombia–Venezuela border.

The fifth installment in the *Déplacé·e·s* project, *Déplacé·e·s, Greece*, takes place on the island of Lesvos. JR and his team gather children from the UNHCR refugee camp to help them unfurl the tarp, which is imprinted with the image of Mozhda, a little girl from Afghanistan. Children and adults carry the tarp throughout the camp, and the procession culminates with a picnic on Lesbos Island.

2023

The exhibition JR - *Déplacé·e·s* debuts at the Gallerie d'Italia in Turin, Italy. Prior to the exhibit opening, JR organizes a procession with all five *Déplacé·e·s* images.

The exhibition *Les Enfants d'Ouranos* opens at Perrotin in New York City.

Giants: Rising Up is installed at Ocean Terminal Deck in Hong Kong's iconic Victoria Harbour.

The *O papel da mão* exhibition opens at Nara Roesler in São Paulo, Brazil.

JR: Chronicles travels to the Lotte Museum of Art in Seoul, South Korea.

The encyclopedic volume of JR's studio artworks, *Artist Until I Find a Real Job*, is released.

JR: *Women* is exhibited at the Pace Gallery in Geneva, Switzerland.

Les Enfants d'Ouranos is installed on the facade of the Parrish Art Museum in Water Mill, New York.

Inside Out Kyiv: We Are Here!, a six-month-long Inside Out Photobooth action, is installed at the PinchukArtCentre in Kyiv, Ukraine.

Retour à la caverne, Act I is installed at the Palais Garnier in Paris, France.

The feature documentary *Tehachapi* has its world premiere at the Telluride Film Festival in New York City.

The *La Ferita* exhibition opens at Galleria Continua in Rome, Italy.

The second installation of *Retour à la caverne, Act II* opens at the Palais Garnier in Paris, France.

Retour à la Caverne - Act II, CHIROPTERA, a project created by JR, Damien Jalet, and Thomas Bangalter, with Amandine Albisson, Étoile dancer of the Opéra national de Paris and 153 dancers from all over the world, is performed in front of the Palais Garnier in Paris, France.

The Chronicles of Miami mural debuts with two installations and a Perrotin exhibition in Miami.

The Machine Behind the Art: Inside JR's Printing Press, an immersive exhibition, opens at Superblue in Miami, Florida.

2024

The exhibition *Tehachapi* opens at Simon Studer Art in Geneva, Switzerland.

La Nascita, a trompe-l'oeil installation across the Piazza Duca d'Aosta in front of the Milano Centrale Railway Station in Italy.

L'Observatoire, a carriage created by JR for the Venice Simplon-Orient-Express train, unveiled during the Venice Biennale.

The exhibition *JR - Déplacées* opens at Kulturhuset Stadsteatern in Stockholm, Sweden.

The exhibition *Dans la lumière* opens at Perrotin in Paris, France.

ACKNOWLEDGMENTS

To JR, my sincere appreciation for sharing your words and thoughts in this publication. It is a continued inspiration to be aligned with your profoundly creative spirit and mind.

My thanks as well to the entire team at the JR Studio and Inside Out Project, who have facilitated production of this publication. Specials thanks to Marc Azoulay, Carmen Herrera Lawrence, Marcelo De Souza Barbosa, Soizic Marceau, Julie Bergon, and Emilie Su.

My sincere appreciation, as always, to the entire team at Princeton University Press, especially Michelle Komie, Christie Henry, Terri O'Prey, Cathy Slovensky, Jacqueline Poirier, Colleen Suljic, Laurie Schlesinger, Cathy Felgar, Jodi Price, Kathryn Stevens, and Annie Miller. We remain extremely grateful to PUP for their continued professionalism, encouragement, and passion for our projects together throughout the years.

Very special thanks to editorial director Fiona Graham for her invaluable organization of this project, and the entire ISMs series. My thanks as well to Vanessa Lee for research assistance.

My sincere thanks as well to Karen Lautanen for her organization aid on this project and many others, and to Steven Rodríguez for his continued support.

Finally, I give all my bottomless gratitude to my amazing wife, Abbey, and to my wonderful children, Justin, Ethan, Ellie, and Jonah for their love and encouragement.

As always, I give endless love and thanks to my mother Judith.

LARRY WARSH

Renowned French artist **JR** creates monumental public art projects that inspire passersby to ask questions and confront their own perceptions. After his first major project *Portrait of a Generation* (2004–6), which challenged stereotypes of Parisian suburban youth, he began working internationally. Whether it be pasting the faces of Israeli and Palestinian people on both sides of the Separation Wall (2007), the eyes of women on train cars in Kibera, Kenya (2009), or a giant toddler peeking over the US–Mexico border fence (2017), JR's larger-than-life installations amplify the stories of everyday people and foster dialogue.

From creating a trompe-l'oeil at the Louvre with 400 volunteers (2019) to pasting alongside incarcerated men in a California maximum-security prison (2019–22), he seeks to involve everyone in the act of artistic creation, hoping to create conversations and drive social change. As of January 2024, his global participatory art project *Inside Out* has empowered more than half a million people to stand up for what they believe in through large-scale black-and-white portraits.

A multimedia artist at his core, JR's accomplishments include a performance with 154 dancers on thirty-meter-high scaffolding on the Palais Garnier in Paris (2023), the Academy Award–nominated documentary *Faces, Places*, co-directed with Agnés Varda (2017), and a video mural exploring the issue of guns in the USA featured on the cover of *Time* magazine (2018). JR also has a rigorous studio art practice, creating gallery artworks that are exhibited internationally. He has had major retrospectives at the Brooklyn Museum (2019) and Maison Européenne de la Photographie (2018) as well as shown artworks and installations at the Venice Biennale (2022), the San Francisco Museum of Modern Art (2019), and the NGV Triennial (2020).

Larry Warsh has been active in the art world for more than thirty years as a publisher and artist-collaborator. An early collector of Keith Haring and Jean-Michel Basquiat, Warsh was a lead organizer for the exhibition *Basquiat: The Unknown Notebooks*, which debuted at the Brooklyn Museum, New York, in 2015, and later traveled to several American museums. He has loaned artworks by Haring and Basquiat from his collection to numerous exhibitions worldwide, and he served as a curatorial consultant on *Keith Haring | Jean-Michel Basquiat: Crossing Lines* for the NGV. The founder of *Museums Magazine*, Warsh has been involved in many publishing projects and is the editor of several other titles published by Princeton University Press, including Jean-Michel Basquiat's *The Notebooks* (2017), *Keith Haring: 31 Subway Drawings* (2021), and two books by Ai Weiwei, *Humanity* (2018) and *Weiwei-isms* (2012). Warsh has served on the board of the Getty Museum Photographs Council and was a founding member of the Basquiat Authentication Committee until its dissolution in 2012.

ILLUSTRATIONS

Frontispiece: JR, Official portrait, 2022 © Grégoire Machavoine.

Page 104: JR, *GIANTS, Kikito and the Border Patrol, Tecate, Mexico – U.S.A.*, 2017 © JR.

ISMs

Larry Warsh, Series Editor

The ISMs series distills the voices of an exciting range of visual artists and designers into captivating, beautifully made books of quotations for a new generation of readers. In turn passionate, inspiring, humorous, witty, and challenging, these collections offer powerful statements on topics ranging from contemporary culture, politics, and race, to creativity, humanity, and the role of art in the world. Books in this series are edited by Larry Warsh and published by Princeton University Press in association with No More Rulers.

Pharrell-isms, Pharrell Williams

Hirst-isms, Damien Hirst

Warhol-isms, Andy Warhol

Arsham-isms, Daniel Arsham

Abloh-isms, Virgil Abloh

Futura-isms, Futura

Haring-isms, Keith Haring

Basquiat-isms, Jean-Michel Basquiat